Tampa Bay

A PHOTOGRAPHIC PORTRAIT

PHOTOGRAPHY BY
ROBERT LA FOLLETTE

NARRATIVE BY
KAREN T. BARTLETT

First published in the United States of America by:

Twin Lights Publishers, Inc.
8 Hale Street
Rockport, Massachusetts 01966
Telephone: (978) 546-7398
http://www.twinlightspub.com

ISBN: 978-1-885435-92-7
ISBN: 1-885435-92-4

10 9 8 7 6 5 4 3 2 1

(jacket front)
Sunshine Skyway Bridge

(jacket back, clockwise from top)
Riverwalk on Hillsborough River, Ybor City TECO
Trolley, and Safety Harbor Marina

(frontispiece)
Pier 60 at sunset, Clearwater Beach

(opposite)
Clearwater Memorial Causeway

One of the most beautiful ways to get "from here
to there" in the Tampa Bay region is the Clearwater
Memorial Causeway. The elegant s-curved four-lane
bridge with four piers spans the Intracoastal
Waterway connecting downtown Clearwater with
Clearwater Beach. Its greenways and scenic over-
looks of the harbor make it a favorite venue for
cyclists and pedestrians.

Book design by:
SYP Design & Production, Inc.
www.sypdesign.com

Printed in China

INTRODUCTION

With its gleaming skyscrapers against a surreal blue sky, encircled by expanses of green and shaded by tropical palms, the approach to the city of Tampa may invoke the awe and exhilaration Dorothy felt at her first view of the Emerald City of Oz. Tampa is a young and vibrant city with deep historic roots. Its bustling financial and business center has lured major corporations from the big northeastern cities and world capitals. The University of Tampa conducts its academic business beneath the dramatic Moorish spires of what once was one of the world's most lavish hotels. Tampa is, among other things, the Spring Training home of the New York Yankees, the home of the Tampa Bay Buccaneers, and the address of the world-class family adventure destination, Busch Gardens.

Due west of Tampa, on a sand-fringed, sun-dappled peninsula between Old Tampa Bay and the Gulf of Mexico, are Clearwater, spring home of the Philadelphia Phillies; and St Petersburg, home of the Tampa Bay Rays and Tampa Bay Lightning. At the turn of the 20th century, The Don CeSar Hotel, that legendary "pink wedding cake" on St. Pete Beach, and the Vinoy, in downtown St. Petersburg, reigned among Florida's glamorous Grande Dames. The crème de la crème of American society wintered there and sailed, played croquet, and attended debutante balls. Restored to their original grandeur, both still rank among North America's finest hotels. Clearwater's Ruth Eckerd Hall hosts world-renowned performers; and St. Pete's Salvador Dali Museum has the largest collection of the artist's works in existence.

Safety Harbor Marina

Just offshore, surrounded by tranquil waters teeming with dolphins and manatees, are unspoiled barrier islands with sugary white stretches of sand that consistently top the lists of the world's most perfect beaches. Some islands are accessible only by boat; others can be reached via bridges so stunning that they are attractions themselves.

With the gift of abundant wildlife comes responsibility, and the communities of Clearwater, St. Petersburg, Tampa and the region have risen to the challenge with expansive rescue and rehabilitation facilities that allow close encounters with rare and fascinating wildlife.

The people of the Tampa Bay region share many priorities, such as their love of public art and preservation of priceless historic buildings. But it is impossible to put a common cultural fingerprint on the region. Just north of Clearwater is a town where Greek is the home language. Tarpon Springs, founded by Greek sponge fishermen, is the sponge fishing capital of the world. Ybor City, the little town with the Cuban accent on the outskirts of Tampa, once was the cigar capital of the world.

Perhaps you've come to close a big business deal, or to while away the days under a beach umbrella. Maybe it's your first visit, or if you're really fortunate, you live here. Whatever has brought you to Tampa Bay, may Robert La Follette's stunning photography on these pages keep the memories fresh until you return.

Delightfully Deco *(opposite)*

An artful addition to Tampa's sophisticated skyline is a colorful enclave of 1930s-era art deco condominiums in the Channelside area. Deco style is notable for its graceful curving lines, glass block, stainless steel, neon colors, sunbursts, and other geometric patterns.

Tampa City Hall *(above)*

Doric columns and balustrades, terra cotta detailing, and a clock tower add distinction to the stately 1915 municipal building designed for the City of Tampa by renowned local architect M. Leo Elliott, who also designed the Cuban Club in Ybor City.

Tampa Convention Center *(pages 8–9)*

The 600,000 square-foot Tampa Convention Center, surrounded by hotels, shops, restaurants, entertainment venues, the cruise terminal, and the Florida Aquarium, makes Tampa one of Florida's most desirable meeting destinations. The nightlife of Ybor City is a trolley ride away.

Riverwalk on Hillsborough River *(above)*

A $40 million project is underway to create a downtown waterfront promenade along the Hillsborough River to connect hotels, offices, and the Tampa Performing Arts Center with shops, restaurants, and attractions. Several parks along the 2.5-mile pathway provide excellent viewing spots for river and portside events.

Moon over Tampa *(opposite)*

The architecturally diverse skyscrapers of downtown Tampa are especially beautiful when illuminated by city lights from below and a cloudless moonlit night above.

Thriving Financial Center *(opposite)*

Mirrored images of the Bank of America, Regions Bank, and Sun Trust buildings on the dramatic glass panels of One Tampa City Center also reflect Tampa's role as the financial center of Florida's Southwest Gulf Coast. When it was built in 1981, the gleaming 38-story One Tampa City Center was Tampa Bay's tallest skyscraper.

Lykes Gaslight Square Park *(above)*

Idyllic temperatures and lush green spaces make downtown Tampa a pleasant city to enjoy a box lunch or take a power walk during the business day. Something is always happening at Lykes Gaslight Square Park.

Trio of Museums and Gardens *(top and bottom)*

Outdoor sculpture, like *Wandering Spirit* by sculptor, John Henry (above), landscapes, history, and art make a compatible trio on the adjacent grounds of the Florida Botanical Gardens, the Gulf Coast Museum of Art, and the Heritage Museum. The Gulf Coast Museum of Art showcases the work of Florida artists and fine Southeastern crafts.

The Heritage Museum preserves the region's cultural heritage through historic buildings dating back to pioneer days. The Florida Botanical Gardens surround the two museums with native and exotic flora and fauna that emphasize the art and beauty of the region.

Solstice *(opposite)*

Standing 28 feet high in swirls of stainless steel at the Bank of America Tower, the dynamic sculpture, *Solstice*, by Charles O. Perry, reflects not just the sun and city lights but also the commitment of Tampa and her citizens to public art.

Sacred Heart Catholic Church

Magnificent grand-scale Romanesque architecture and old world detailing make the
Sacred Heart Catholic Church, circa 1905,
one of Tampa's finest historic buildings.
The church, with its intricate stained glass
windows, carrera marble altar, and 135-foot
dome, hosts noonday tours once a month,
September through April.

Bayshore Boulevard *(top)*

Flanked on one side by Tampa Bay and on the other by gracious homes on meticulously tended grounds, Bayshore Boulevard is the route of the annual Gasparilla Pirate Invasion parade and home to the world's longest continuous sidewalk of 4.5 miles. It borders the historic Hyde Park residential, shopping and dining district.

MacDill Air Force Base *(bottom)*

Since 1938, when it opened as a training facility for World War II airmen, MacDill Air Force base has been an integral part of the Tampa community. About 6,000 military and civilian personnel work on the 5,000-acre base just south of downtown Tampa.

Emerald City *(pages 18–19)*

With its gleaming skyscrapers against a surreal blue sky, encircled by expanses of green
and shaded by tropical palms, the approach
to the city of Tampa may invoke the awe
and exhilaration Dorothy felt at her first
view of the Emerald City of Oz.

Legends Field *(above)*

The spring home of the New York Yankees
since 1996, the 31-acre Legends Field is
identical in field dimensions to Yankee
Stadium. More than 200,000 fans flock to
this field during spring training to watch
the Yankees warm up for the coming season.

BABE RUTH

UNIFORM NUMBER RETIRED: 1948

FROM 1920-1934, BABE SINGLEHANDEDLY LIFTED BASEBALL TO NEW HEIGHTS WITH HIS ULTIMATE TALENT AND UNBRIDLED LOVE FOR THE GAME. HIS ENORMOUS CONTRIBUTIONS TO BASEBALL AND THE YANKEES MADE HIM THE MOST CELEBRATED ATHLETE WHO EVER LIVED

Monument Park, Tropical Style *(top)*

Yankees numbers 3 (Ruth), 7 (Mantle), 8 (Berra), 37 (Stengel), 9 (Maris), 4 (Gehrig), and ten other venerable numbers are engraved on the hearts of diehard Yankees fans. The owners of those 16 retired numbers are honored with plaques among the palm trees at Tampa's tropical version of Monument Park in New York's Yankee Stadium.

VIP, Yankee Stadium *(bottom)*

Among the newest features of the 10,000-seat stadium is the Bright House Networks' Dugout Club, an exclusive seating area and lounge behind home plate and a 23-suite private club under the stands. The 31-acre complex on Steinbrenner Drive also hosts winter fantasy camps with Yankee coaches and team members.

Tampa Bay Downs

Kentucky Derby winners and trainers have raced and trained at Tampa Bay Downs. Dating back to 1926, it is among the oldest and best maintained thoroughbred horse tracks in the United States and one of the most popular turf courses in North America.

And...They're Off!

The season for the "Sport of Kings" at Tampa Bay Downs runs from December to May, with simulcasts on non-racing days, monthly festivals, and more than $2.5 million in stakes purses. Multi-taskers can practice their golf swings or slip in a couple of rounds at the Silks Poker Room while waiting for the next race.

University of South Florida *(top)*

The new award-winning University of South Florida Intercollegiate Athletic Facility, with its dramatic green steel beams and reflective windows, is a focal point of the contemporary USF campus. The space features state-of-the-art athletic training equipment, including an underwater treadmill.

USF Sun Dome *(bottom)*

Noted for its futuristic steel dome that soars 115 feet above the arena floor, the USF Sun Dome is home to the South Florida Bulls basketball and volleyball teams. The 55,000 square-foot arena, with a capacity of more than 11,000 people, also hosts concerts and other events.

A Leading Research University *(opposite)*

USF serves more than 45,000 students on its home campus of Tampa and on three other campuses: St. Petersburg, Sarasota-Manatee, and Lakeland. It is the ninth largest public university in the United States, and among the top-ranked public research universities in the country.

University of Tampa *(top)*

Set on 100 acres of the most valuable and vibrant real estate on Tampa Bay, the University of Tampa is headquartered in what once was the glamorous Tampa Bay Hotel, dating back to Florida's Gilded Age at the turn of the 20th century. The private liberal arts college serves approximately 5,500 students in 48 buildings.

Sticks of Fire *(bottom)*

The Calusa Indians named this region Tampa, meaning "Sticks of Fire", in reference either to the prevalence of quick-burning driftwood on area beaches, or the frequent phenomenon of lightning that has earned Tampa Bay the designation as the lightning capital of North America. The *Sticks of Fire* sculpture by Stephanie Trip graces the UT campus.

Beneath the UT Dome *(opposite)*

The south wing of Plant Hall, beneath the dome of the circa 1891 Tampa Bay Hotel, is now a museum preserving the legacy of railroad magnate Henry Plant. His glitzy hotel was a center of Florida's winter social scene enjoyed by rich and famous guests, the likes of Sarah Bernhardt, Teddy Roosevelt, and Babe Ruth.

Tampa Port Authority *(top)*

Nearly one million passengers cruise in and out of the Port of Tampa annually. Its combined passenger and cruise commerce make it Florida's largest port. Tampa offers the most direct passenger routes to Mexico, Latin America, and the Caribbean. Homeport lines include Carnival, Royal Caribbean, and Holland America.

Channelside Bay Plaza *(bottom)*

An extra perk for cruise passengers is the adjacent Channelside Bay Plaza, the answer to a last-minute shopper's prayers. Also a popular nightspot for locals and land-side visitors, Channelside offers casual and elegant dining, entertainment, and events.

Remember When *(opposite)*

In 1926, flashbulb-style movie lights were illuminated for the first time on the seven-story sign over Tampa's glam new movie palace. During the 1950's, children could see a movie at Tampa Theatre for 25 cents and six RC-Cola bottle caps. Nearly 80 years later, the restored landmark is a nostalgic venue for classic films, concerts, and special events.

Weird Science

Anyone who envisions science and industry as the stuff of dusty lecture halls hasn't been to Tampa's Museum of Science and Industry. MOSI is a dynamic, multi-sensory experience that transforms ordinary spectators into daredevils and wizards. The journey begins at the skeletal feet of a three-story-high diplodocus dinosaur.

MOSI at Night

The dramatically night-lighted IMAX dome offers tantalizing promise of the wonders within the walls of MOSI. Visitors can pedal a bicycle across a one-inch steel high wire suspended 30 feet above the floor, step into a virtual hurricane, and examine the craters of the moon in the state-of-the-art planetarium.

BioWorks Butterfly Garden *(top)*

MOSI's BioWorks Butterfly Garden encompasses the gardens and ponds of a natural butterfly habitat and animal husbandry laboratory where guests can watch the butterfly life cycle from egg to adult. The engineered ecosystem demonstrates nature's own wastewater cleaning capabilities as an alternative to man-made wastewater treatment systems.

Florida Monarch *(bottom)*

The BioWorks Butterfly Garden rears only butterflies native to Florida. The non-migrating Florida monarch butterfly varies slightly from the migratory monarchs that fly each autumn from eastern North America to central Mexico. When a Florida monarch is at rest, observers can tell the male from the female by the black spots on the male's lower wings.

Tampa Museum of Art

With an ever-expanding collection of fine 20th-century art, contemporary work, and Greek and Roman antiquities, the Tampa Museum of Art has outgrown its current facilities. Plans are underway for a spectacular new 120,000 square foot contemporary museum in Curtis Hixon Park on the Hillsborough River.

Union Station (top)

Since 1912, when boxcars took loads of citrus north, and passenger cars brought wintering socialites south, the Italian Renaissance train depot has been an important Tampa gateway. After a 20-year slide into disrepair, the venerable old station was restored in 1998. It now is a stop on Amtrak's Silver Service between Miami and New York.

Florida Avenue Postcard (bottom)

The largest postcard in Tampa Bay is the beloved Carl Cowden mural at the corner of Florida Avenue at Royal Street. Within the letters spelling TAMPA are historic scenes and present-day landmarks, including the Sulfur Springs water tower, a minaret rising from The University of Tampa campus, and an Ybor City streetcar.

Centennial Clock Keep (opposite)

Sculptor William Culbertson designed the clock tower at Union Station to depict cultural and historical symbols of Tampa Bay's golden age of rail travel. The capstone at the top resembles the tower that once housed the watchman who operated the crossing gate. Union Station is listed on the National Register of Historic Places.

Restoring the Fenway

In the 1920s, the Fenway Hotel, overlooking Caladesi Sound, was the pride of Dunedin. Her prominent guests played croquet and tennis and attended teas and dances. Since the1960s, it has been the campus of two colleges, and, in 2007, the "Once Grand Lady of the Bay" was purchased by a private preservationist/investor with plans for restoration.

Henry B. Plant Museum

A Moorish keyhole entry and Victorian ginger-bread trim welcome visitors to Plant Hall, the southeast wing of Henry B. Plant's opulent 1891 Tampa Bay Hotel. The historic landmark hotel now is the cornerstone building of the University of Tampa. The Henry B. Plant Museum in Plant Hall preserves and displays artifacts from the hotel's glamour days.

U.S. Coast Guard Rescue *(top)*

The U.S. Coast Guard conducts some of its most intense training operations in Tampa Bay. The elite team in the bright red and white helicopters and boats are prepared to respond to toxic spills, storm rescue, and vessels that have run aground. The Tampa unit was involved in saving lives in the aftermath of Hurricane Katrina.

Boating Safety *(bottom)*

In addition to its rescue operations, the local Tampa unit gives classes in boating safety. According to U.S. Coast Guard statistics, every day its National Boating Safety Division saves 10 lives, assists 192 people in distress, protects $2.7 million in property, seizes 475 pounds of illegal drugs worth $10 million, and investigates 6 vessel casualties.

Sulphur Springs Water Tower *(opposite)*

The 214-foot tall tower was built in 1927 for the Sulphur Springs Hotel and Arcade, where the wealthy came to partake of the "miraculous healing waters." After falling into disrepair, it found new life in the 1970s as a drive-in theater, and recently as the focal point of the City of Tampa's new River Tower Park.

Tampa Performing Arts Center

From Broadway and grand opera to rock concerts and symphonies, the world class performing arts center, in downtown Tampa, claims the title of the largest such facility south of New York's Kennedy Center. In its two-decade history, it has logged an audience count of ten million people. Tampa Bay Performing Arts Center consists of five theaters, a performing arts conservatory, and a rehearsal hall, as well as boutiques and restaurants.

American Victory Museum

One of only two 534 Victory merchant marine cargo ships still sailing, *American Victory* was commissioned during World War I, the Korean War and Vietnam. It now is a floating museum featuring collections of weaponry, uniforms and artifacts. A tour of the ship includes the flying bridge, wheelhouse, and more.

Columbia Restaurant

Acclaimed traditional Spanish cuisine, including tapas, wines, and sherries are just part of the early 20th-century ambience of the Hernandez-Gonzmart family restaurant that has grown to seven locations throughout Florida. The Old World period architecture and nightly flamenco shows make dining in the Ybor City restaurant a cultural trip back in time.

Crafted in Spain *(top)*

Thought to be the world's largest Spanish restaurant, the Columbia is an architectural treasure of hand-painted tiles, heavy chandeliers, ancient wrought iron, and wood detailing crafted in Spain. Cervantes' larger-than-life fictional knight-errant, Don Quixote, and his sidekick, Sancho Panza, are depicted in intricate tilework on the building's façade.

Hand-Rolled Cigars *(bottom)*

Ybor City, one of Florida's two Historic Landmark Districts, was founded by Cuban cigar makers who left Key West for a better life. At its heyday, Ybor City and neighboring Tampa had 140 cigar factories. Today in Ybor City a handful of cigar shops still offer hand-rolled cigars, often made by the great grandchildren of the founders.

Ybor City Museum *(top)*

The neighborhood Ferlita Bakery was opened in 1896 by Sicilian immigrant Francisco Ferlita and operated by his descendants until Ybor city fell onto hard times in the 1970s. The bakery building was acquired by the Florida State Park Service and restored as part of the Ybor City Museum complex celebrating the city's ethnic heritage.

TECO Trolley *(bottom)*

Late 1800s cigar workers took electric streetcars to their factory jobs. Later, families rode them downtown to baseball games. Sadly, the streetcar bells clanged for the last time after World War II, remaining silent until the TECO line opened with fanfare in 2002, connecting downtown Tampa, Channelside, and Ybor City.

Honoring Immigrants *(opposite)*

Noted Tampa bronze sculptor, Steven Dickey was commissioned to create the poignant statue of an immigrant family in Ybor City's Centennial Park to honor the men and women who came to this country in search of personal freedom, economic opportunity, and a future of hope for their families.

Ybor City Lights (above)

The reflections of old-fashioned street lamps and vibrant neon signs from the clubs, restaurants, and boutiques of Ybor city also reflect the energy of a revitalized historic district. Weekdays are tranquil, as though the city is resting up for the young Friday and Saturday night revelers.

Centro Ybor (opposite)

The Cuban-themed Muvico Centro Ybor and the restored historic Centro Ybor building set the tone for Ybor's all-inclusive entertainment complex, which includes restaurants, shops, clubs, and 20 movie screens.

Casitas *(left)*

Tiny three-room "shotgun" houses—so named because the central hallway would allow a bullet to pass from the front door to the back —housed the families of Cuban cigar workers in the 1880s. Seven of the original casitas, with their gingerbread-trimmed porches, have been relocated to 9th Avenue East as part of the Ybor City Museum complex.

Don Vicente Martinez Ybor *(right)*

In 1885, Spanish-American industrialist and cigar magnate Don Vicente Martinez Ybor turned swampland into a factory town that would become the cigar capital of the world. He also built the first casitas in antici-pation of the more than 3,000 workers who would arrive within the first year. The bronze statue is by Steven Dickey.

Cuban Immigrant Mural

Sociedad La Union Marti-Maceo, named for
its founders, Jose Marti and General Antonio
Mateo, was a club for Afro-Cuban cigar workers
who migrated to Ybor City in the early 1900s.
Current members include multi-generational
descendents of the original members. The
colorful mural graces the side of the club
building at 1226 La Septima (7th Avenue).

Serengeti Express

The bright green and red steam engine at Busch Gardens, a replica of 1900s-era African trains, circles the two-mile perimeter of the park's African habitats. The open cars allow unobstructed animal views and an excellent vantage point to observe the park's world-famous mammoth coasters.

Ringtail Lemur *(top)*

The female-dominated troops of tree-dwellers are fun to watch as they savor their meals of fresh fruit and sun themselves in their habitat at Busch Gardens' Edge of Africa.

Myombe Reserve *(bottom)*

Busch Gardens' Myombe Reserve provides the perfect opportunity to observe these endangered knuckle-walking pan troglodytes, which are native to West and Central Africa. Geneticists say that the chimpanzee is a human being's closest living relative, sharing about 98 percent of our DNA.

White Bengal Tiger (opposite)

The rare white Bengal tiger is the second largest cat in the world, with a possible weight of up to 450 pounds. They are extremely beautiful with their blue eyes and chocolate stripes. These extraordinary white tigers can be seen at Busch Gardens' Jungala.

Endangered Zebra (top)

Zebras live in harmony with giraffes, gazelles, impalas and other African species in a re-created natural habitat on Busch Gardens' Serengeti Plain. A dramatic brown and white, Grevy's Zebras are native to eastern Africa. Once hunted for their beautiful skins, they have become endangered in this century due to loss of habitat.

Pink Flamingo (bottom)

The flamingo lagoon at Busch Gardens has a population of more than 100 birds. Their long legs and bright pink feathers make a colony of pink flamingoes among the most photogenic bird scenes in the world. Their coloring comes from the alpha and beta-carotene in the shrimp and other seafood in their diets.

Ibis *(left)*

Considered sacred in ancient Egyptian cultures, ibis are recognizable by their orange legs and long, curved bills which turn bright red/orange during breeding season. Ibis make an impressive sight feeding in groups on wet grass, mangroves, and along the seashore. The immature ibis is gray; the adult is pure white.

Anhinga *(right)*

Sometimes called water turkeys or snake birds because they submerge themselves and swim with only their long necks out of the water, Anhingas must allow their feathers to dry completely before they can fly. The black birds with silver feather markings can be spotted sunning themselves with out-stretched wings on rocks and grassy areas.

Brown Anole *(opposite)*

Introduced to the U.S. from Cuba in the mid 20th century, the anole is one of 36 species of non-native lizards. Shy but gentle and curious, anoles often allow humans to get close enough to observe the tiny wide footpads that allow them to cling to flat surfaces.

American Bald Eagle *(opposite)*

The American Bald Eagle is a large raptor with a wingspan of up to seven feet, talons up to four inches long, and a diving speed of 100-plus miles per hour. These natural hunters feed on fish, waterfowl, turtles, and small mammals. They acquire their distinctive white head feathers at age five or six years.

Osprey *(top)*

Resembling, but not quite as large as the American Bald Eagle, the osprey is a fish-eating raptor that often is seen nesting atop dead trees, power poles, and channel markers. Boaters can see hatchlings in the nests during the primary nesting season between February and June.

Red-Shouldered Hawk *(above)*

Lucky sightings of the graceful Red-shouldered Hawk typically occur near their woodland habitats or over open water. This one was spotted on the fringe of the 8,500-acre Brooker Creek Preserve in the northeastern corner of Pinellas County. Soaring on a 40-inch wingspan, the Red-shouldered Hawk hunts insects, small mammals, and reptiles.

Tampa's Lowry Park Zoo *(top)*

Though it started in the 1950s as a collection of exotic animals, Tampa's Lowry Park Zoo now is a steward of endangered and threatened species, a habitat for regional wildlife, and a great place for kids to play in an animal-themed environment. The zoo's 56 acres include shows, rides, and two water play areas.

Mermaid or Elephant? *(bottom)*

The shy, slow-moving West Indian Manatee, is related to the elephant; and although she more closely resembles her common name, "sea cow," drunken sailors of earlier centuries did mistake manatees for Sirens: sensuous mermaid-like creatures from Greek mythology whose songs lured ships to their doom on the rocks.

Dark Continent Experiences *(opposite)*

Those longing to get up close and personal with white rhinos, African elephants, crocodiles, and giraffes need never leave Tampa Bay. They can just check out Safari Africa at Tampa's Lowry Park Zoo or Busch Gardens' Edge of Africa, where they can hand-feed giraffes from the back of an open vehicle.

Safari Africa

Enter the tunnel in Tampa and emerge on the African continent, at Safari Africa, the newest section of Tampa's Lowry Park Zoo. Take a behind-the-scenes safari ride to commune with elephants, zebras, meerkats, and more. After exploring Africa, an Australian-themed habitat awaits, where you can pet a stingray at the zoo's Stingray Bay.

Giving a Hoot

Tampa's Lowry Park Zoo has more than 2,000 animals in habitats and ecosystems ranging from Penguin Beach to Primate World. Jeff the Zoo Guy, along with his team of Zoo Ambassadors, is a regular on talk shows and wildlife documentaries. Among Jeff's favorites is the noisy-but-cute Barred Owl, also known as the Hoot Owl.

Diving with the Sharks *(top)*

The Florida Aquarium provides shark cages (for the people, not the sharks) plus SCUBA gear and personal dive masters for those who dare to descend into this 93,000-gallon salt-water habitat, where tiger sharks, nurse sharks, zebra sharks, and black-tip reef sharks swim with, among other creatures, giant green turtles and large schools of yellowtail fish.

Dolphins in the Wild *(bottom)*

There are more than 400 Atlantic bottlenose dolphins in Tampa Bay, and the Florida Aquarium's 64-foot catamaran, *Bay Spirit*, takes up to 49 guests at a time into Tampa Bay to see them in the wild.

Florida Aquarium

The penguins promenade twice daily at ten and three; kids can crawl into a giant hermit crab shell; there's the "no-bone-zone" to find out what boneless sea creatures like sea stars, crabs, and giant clams feel like, and some honest to goodness sea dragons. What more could a kid (of any age) want?

Winter Lives Here *(top)*

The three-month-old female Atlantic bot-tlenose dolphin was found entangled in a crab trap with deep wounds, and partially destroyed tail. Winter was not expected to live, but with dedicated care , she's now a thriving and beloved member of the CMA family. Her plight and rescue caught the attention of the entire dolphin rescue world.

Trainer for a Day *(bottom)*

The Clearwater Marine Aquarium rescues sick and injured animals, rehabilitates and releases most back to their natural habitats, and permanently cares for those whose injuries do not allow their safe release. CMA also offers animal and dolphin encounters, behind the scenes tours, and a "trainer for a day" program for kids ages 8 – 11.

Green Turtle *(opposite)*

Hundreds of female turtles (Loggerheads, Hawksbills, Kemps Riddles and Green Turtles like this one) return each year to the same nesting spot on a beach in the Tampa Bay area to lay up to 200 eggs. The Clearwater Marine Aquarium monitors nesting and hatch data, and offers an adopt-a-turtle pro-gram to help support the rescue missions.

Suncoast Seabird Sanctuary *(opposite)*

Rescue and rehabilitation is the mission of the Suncoast Seabird Sanctuary, the largest wild bird hospital and rehabilitation center in the U.S. At least 7,500 injured birds are admitted annually, with at least 600 in residence at a time. The non-profit center is supported entirely by donations, adoptions, and volunteer workers. Admission is free.

Tri-colored Heron *(top)*

Also known as the Louisiana Heron, the Tri-colored Heron is a more delicate version of the Great Blue Heron. Its favorite state is Florida, where they are easy to spot throughout the Tampa Bay area.

Reddish Egret *(bottom)*

While the Reddish Egret comes by its name honestly, it's just as likely that a hatchling in the same nest will turn out white. Reddish Egrets catch their fish by spreading their wings over the water to provide shade for unsuspecting prey.

Palm Gardens at Florida Botanical

More than 150 types of birds, mammals, and reptiles have been documented at the Florida Botanical Gardens. The showcase gardens and undisturbed habitats of wetlands, scrublands and forests, plus a gift shop and educational facilities, encompass 160,000 acres under the Florida Botanical Gardens' care. Admission is free.

Yellow Jessamine *(top)*

The strong evergreen vine with the bright yellow blossoms and shiny green leaves can be seen winding up trellises and around mailboxes all over Tampa Bay. But be warned: its lovely fragrance and beneficial use in hair products belies its poisonous nature.

Water Lily *(bottom)*

The exotic blooms of the water lily are at their best upon opening in the early morning. Water lilies thrive especially well in the still ponds at the Florida Botanical Gardens.

Florida Botanical Gardens *(top)*

Rose, topiary, and palm gardens are just a few of the stunning landscapes of the Florida Botanical Gardens, which provide habitats for more than 150 types of wildlife species. The Tropical Fruit Garden showcases the luscious papayas, mangos, bananas, citrus, and other fruits that thrive in the subtropical climate of the Tampa Bay region.

Bougainvillea *(bottom)*

Bougainvillea is an ever-present reminder of the joy of living in a semi-tropical environment. The vivid displays of red, purple, and orange blooms on lush vines are seen spilling over walls, draped over archways, and even trained as hedges and topiary.

Pickerel Weed *(opposite)*

Captured by the lens at the Florida Botanical Gardens, this spiky blue relative of the water hyacinth also grows abundantly in swamps, lagoons, ponds, and still wetlands throughout Florida's Gulf Coast.

Clearwater Beach *(top)*

The name of both the beach and the island it fringes, Clearwater Beach is just three miles long and four blocks wide. The end-to-end umbrellas, beach volleyball courts, water sports, concessions, and lounging sun-worshippers attest to the popularity of this tiny island's tranquil waters and soft white sands.

Breakfast on the Beach *(bottom)*

This baby Black Skimmer has not yet gotten its trademark black and white suit or the dramatic red-banded bill and legs of its parents. Black Skimmers lounge and play on beaches and dunes during the day and forage by skimming shallow waters for small fish and crustaceans at dawn and dusk.

Pass-a-Grille *(opposite)*

Despite its original fancy name of Passe aux Grilleurs (French for Pirate's Pass) and its proximity to the glamorous Don CeSar Hotel on St. Pete Beach, the Old Florida village of Pass-a-Grille's best claim to fame may be the huge school of whales that beached themselves in 1946 and the gentle sea oats-covered dunes.

Pier 60

Among the prettiest and best-equipped fishing piers in the Tampa Bay area, Pier 60 is popular for morning strolls and mid-day beach breaks. There is a food concession and a gift shop, and the pier affords panoramic views of Clearwater Beach. At day's end, crowds gather for the Key West-style sunset celebration with jugglers, mimes, music, and food.

Clearwater Beach

The meticulously-maintained Pier 60 Park at Clearwater Beach is among the region's favorite family spots for watersports, Frisbee-tossing, sand castle-building, and napping in the shade of umbrellas. There are food concessions, a bait shop, and a covered playground on the sand.

Surfing on Gulf of Mexico *(top)*

Despite its usually-tranquil waters, the Gulf of
Mexico can surprise and delight surfers with
respectable breakers, especially in winter,
from offshore east/northeastern winds; and
from the effects of summer storms originat-
ing in the Caribbean, as happened one
recent summer day.

Seagull's Eye View *(opposite)*

Crystal blue swimming pools, three miles of
walking beaches, and artful rows of palms in
sugary white sand lure vacationers year after
year to the hotels and motels overlooking
Clearwater Beach.

Cleveland Street *(opposite)*

The splashy reds and yellows on this downtown Clearwater building are sure to bring
smiles to the faces of those strolling down
Cleveland Street. Once the bustling center
of Clearwater, Cleveland Street's recent
$9 million downtown revitalization project
included public art, landscaping and
pedestrian-friendly enhancements.

City of Murals *(above)*

Commissioned by Friends of Clearwater, the
delightful mural depicting a pastoral
Mediterranean cottage scene at the corner
of Cleveland Street at Garden is an example
of the public art that graces many Tampa
Bay streetscapes.

White Queen of the Gulf

Just south of downtown Clearwater on the
Intracoastal Waterway, a grand old hotel
affectionately called The White Queen of
the Gulf dates back to the days of luxury rail
travel and society debutante balls. Currently
named the Belleview Biltmore, the old hotel
has been acquired by a preservationist/
developer with plans to restore it.

Clearwater City Hall *(top)*

Clearwater's City Hall, located directly across from Pier 60 on Osceola Avenue, sponsors an aggressive program of public art and operates webcams from Clearwater Beach and Pier 60. In addition to housing the city's municipal offices, Clearwater City Hall is often the site of arts exhibitions and concerts sponsored by the Clearwater Arts Foundation.

Pinellas County Courthouse *(bottom)*

Built in 1918 in Classic Revival style, this gracious structure in Clearwater is the seat of government for Pinellas County, which occupies the large peninsula on the west side of Tampa Bay. The major towns in Pinellas County are Clearwater, Largo, St. Petersburg, and Tarpon Springs.

Island Hopping *(top)*

Boaters have vast choices for spending an hour, a day, or a weekend on the water, from the open Gulf of Mexico to sheltered bays and rivers. Two nearby islands popular with boaters are Caladesi Island, just west of the Dunedin Causeway Bridge, and Honeymoon Island to the north of Caladesi.

Blueways *(bottom)*

Both Hillsborough and Pinellas Counties offer paddlers a vast system of Blueways: specially mapped trails through creeks, rivers, bays, and estuaries. The calm waters around the Clearwater Memorial Causeway at Dunedin make this area a favored passage for kayakers. Canoes, kayaks, and full outfitting rentals are widely available.

Captain Memo's Pirate Ship *(opposite)*

If dastardly pirates, salty seadogs, and loud cannons firing from the deck of a "real" pirate ship weren't excitement enough, kids get their own hats and goodies on Captain Memo's bright red, 125-passenger sightseeing ship, *Pirate's Ransom*. There are sunset and sightseeing cruises and theme parties for adults too.

John's Pass

Surprisingly little has changed over the years
at this turn-of-the-20th century fishing village on Madeira Beach between Clearwater
and St. Petersburg. John's Pass is still the
headquarters for a local fishing fleet, as well
as parasailing and other watersports vendors.

Seafood and Pirate Invasions

More than 100 restaurants and shops, offering everything from ice cream and fresh seafood to fine crafts and kitschy treasures, are packed end-to-end in the village. Funky "Old Florida" weekend festivals lure huge crowds, as do the annual October John's Pass Seafood Festival, and the John Levique Pirate Invasion each June.

Hillsborough River Park *(opposite)*

One of Florida's first state parks, this natural reserve includes several ecosystems, including oak hammocks, wetlands trails, the river, and even Florida-style "rapids." The park offers canoe and kayak rentals, fishing, camping, and picnic sites. Photo opportunities abound, including the replica of a fort from the Second Seminole War and a wooden bridge.

Basking Turtle *(top)*

Commonly called the Cooter Turtle, these little guys prefer the still waters of ponds and backwaters, and can be most often seen either sunning themselves on rocks or floating with just their heads breaking the water. Cooters average less than 12 inches long.

Alligator *(bottom)*

Alligator sightings can occur anywhere there's a body of fresh or brackish (part salt, part fresh) water: marshlands, lakes, rivers, swamps, ponds; even golf course water hazards. How to tell an alligator from a crocodile? Gators have broad, short snouts; crocs have long, sharper snouts and their teeth show when the mouth is closed.

Sunset on Honeymoon Island

Hog Island, as the pioneers named it, just didn't seem right for one of the most pristine, romantic islands on the Gulf of Mexico, so an ambitious developer changed it to Honeymoon Island. Now a Florida State Park, the best-kept secret has miles of shelling beaches, a virgin forest, a vast bird population, and a new nature center.

Fireworks (*above*)

Dozens of 4th of July and New Year's Eve fireworks extravaganzas take place all over the Tampa Bay region. Among the largest is the one launched from the Clearwater Memorial Causeway. The water magnifies the heart-racing sound of each explosion, and the brilliant colors are visible for miles.

Greek Fishing Village (*opposite*)

Around the turn of the last century, a mother lode of natural sponge was discovered in the Gulf of Mexico, and Greek sponge fishermen migrated from the exotic Dodecanese Islands to settle in the little town of Tarpon Springs. Today, the docks along the Anclote River still exude the ambience of an Old World Greek sponge-fishing village.

Sponge Capital of the World (top)

A larger-than-life bronze statue at the docks on the Anclote River honors the first Greek sponge fishermen who arrived in Tarpon Springs a century ago. By the 1930s, Tarpon Springs had become the sponge fishing capital of the world, and it holds that title today.

Shopping for Sponges (bottom)

Along with the swarthy fishermen, whose descendants still speak the native tongue, came authentic Greek bakeries, coffee shops, and handicrafts, which still lure visitors today, not just to buy natural sponges, but also to sample the rich Tarpon Springs culture.

The Yachting Life (opposite)

With its sheltered and open-water boating venues, year-round sunshine, and more than enough wind to fill the sails—both practically and spiritually—the Tampa Bay area is a mariner's dream. The hundreds of charter companies and brokers, spectacular boat shows, and waiting lists for slips at the marinas prove the point.

Clearwater Marina (top)

The 220-slip Clearwater Municipal Marina, across from Pier 60, is home to the largest fishing fleet on the west coast of Florida. It is home base for fishing and sailing charters, sightseeing boats, dinner cruises, dolphin tours, parasailing, and personal watercraft rentals.

Along the Intracoastal Waterway (bottom)

The Gulf Coast of Florida's blue skies, aqua-marine waters, and gentle seaside lifestyle draw many comparisons to the Mediterranean Sea. The Italian influence is particularly notable in the architecture, which features red clay tile roofs and broad loggias and verandas to catch the Gulf breezes.

Sunfish Sailing (opposite)

One needn't have a yacht to experience the exhilaration of sailing. Sunfish and Sailfish, canoe and kayak rentals, and a range of personal watercraft are available at piers, marinas, and beach resorts.

McMullen Log Cabin *(top)*

Heritage Village, a living history museum set into a natural scrub and palmetto landscape, is reminiscent of Florida as it was nearly 150 years ago. The 1868 McMullen House, log cabin of Largo pioneer Daniel McMullen, is the oldest structure in the county. It is said that more than 55 babies were born in the cabin.

Heritage Mercantile *(bottom)*

Originally a neighborhood grocery store and meat market in St. Petersburg, the historic building was acquired by the City of St. Petersburg and moved to its present site at Heritage Village. It has been restored as a 1920s-era general store with a gas station and garage.

1920s Garage

The Pin-Mar Antique Car Club of Pinellas County was instrumental in the restoration of Heritage Mercantile and hosts antique auto events on the property. Among the other historic properties relocated to Heritage Village are a sponge warehouse, a bandstand, a church, a school, a railroad depot, and even outhouses.

Ruth Eckerd Hall *(top)*

Clearwater's classy, acoustically superior performing arts hall and its Marcia P. Hoffman Performing Arts Institute play host to nearly half a million people each year, for performances ranging from Broadway musicals to stage dramas, pops concerts and dance productions, and for education in the performing arts.

Bright House Networks Field *(bottom)*

Modest prices, a great location off U.S. 19 and fine Philadelphia cheese steaks make this colorful new, family-friendly, 8,500-capacity ball park in Clearwater a great place to see the Philadelphia Phillies in spring training. The Phillies have made Clearwater their spring home since 1947.

Lefty Grove *(opposite)*

Phillies star Lefty Grove, one of the greatest pitchers in history, was said to be right-handed off the field. Phillies lore says he used his right hand to punch lockers. Grove, who won seven strikeout titles and four World Series games, was inducted into the Baseball Hall of Fame in 1947. He is immortalized in bronze at Bright House Networks Field.

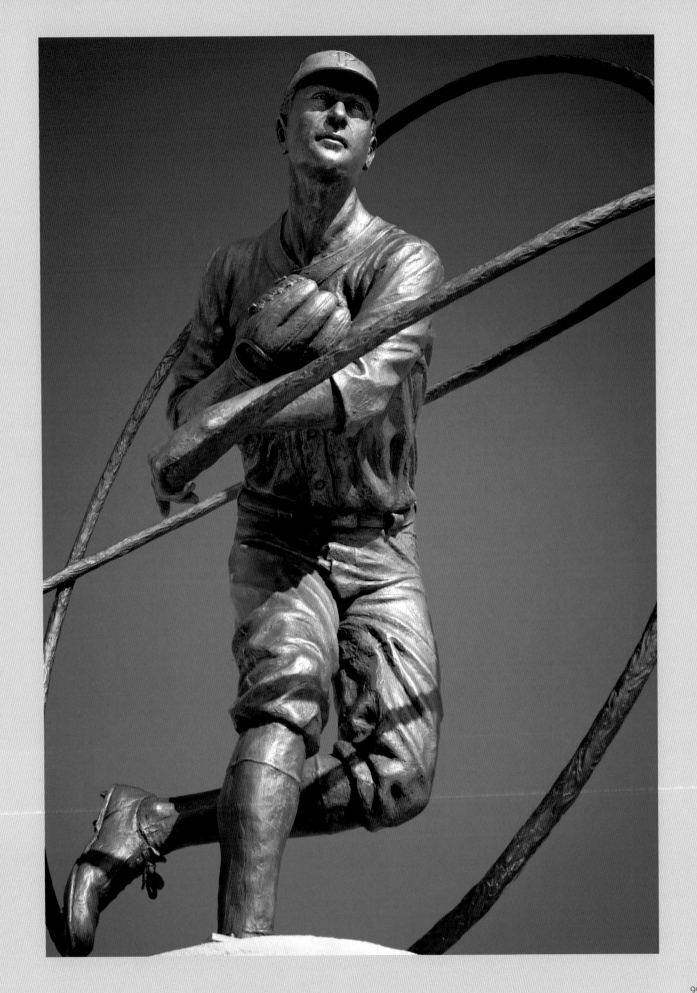

Tropicana Field *(top and opposite)*

Long-time visitors and residents may remember it as the Florida Suncoast Dome or the Thunder Dome, featuring the world's second-largest cable-supported domed roof. The current incarnation of this 1.1 million square-foot professional sports facility is called Tropicana Field, but that may change when the resident professional baseball team, the Tampa Bay Rays, build their proposed new stadium in downtown St. Pete. For now, fans of the feisty Rays (formerly the Devil Rays) still enjoy the 10,000 gallon tank where they can pet and feed Cownose Rays while they cheer their team.

St. Pete Times Forum *(bottom)*

75-foot tall lightning bolts welcome fans to the home of the Tampa Bay Lightning professional hockey team. The 20,000-seat St. Pete Times Forum arena also is the venue for big name concerts, ice shows, circus extravaganzas, and sporting events.

Dunedin Marina

For those arriving by boat, the pretty
Dunedin Marina, with nearly 200 wet slips,
is located on the Intracoastal Waterway
between the Dunedin and Clearwater
causeways, east of channel markers #4 and
#5. The marina is home to one of Florida's
oldest sailing clubs, which has an active
cruising and racing calendar.

Pier Bait House

Pelicans are such regulars on St. Pete's pier that the Bait House staffers have names for many of them. Henrietta has been flying in for her herring-and-sardine lunch for 27 years, and this un-named rescued-and-released bird from the Seabird Sanctuary likes to stand at the Bait House door and stare at Bonnie, his new best friend.

Vinoy Park

Sophisticated high-rise residential towers, an expansive public park, and the glamorous Vinoy Resort overlook the historic yacht harbor in Vinoy Basin. With its Mediterranean-style ambience and green open spaces, Vinoy Basin, also known as Vinoy Park, is a popular setting for concerts, fireworks, art shows, and gatherings in Downtown St. Petersburg.

Great Egret

Great Egrets, Snowy Egrets, and Great White Herons are all abundant in the Tampa Bay area. They can be seen on beaches, in mangroves, marshes, and ponds. The Great Egret is recognizable by his green eye bands, bright yellow beak, and black legs.

The Pier (top and bottom)

Natives may still call it the Million Dollar Pier, built in 1926 to replace the original Pier Pavilion built in 1895. Today, it's called simply The Pier, but there's nothing simple about this playful, Crayon box-colored five-story inverted pyramid structure teeming with, shops, galleries, restaurants, and tiki bars; or its boardwalk crowded with fishermen, tourists, sightseeing and fishing charters, and watersport rentals. The Pier even has its own 2,000 square foot aquarium where, among other things, humans can listen as sea creatures communicate with each other.

Downtown St. Pete

The Pier is a prime vantage point to enjoy a view of downtown St. Petersburg. The Pier and its observation deck are also the places to be to view fireworks shows and holiday boat parades. Visitors can park in the adjacent lots and take one of the free bright red trolleys up the boulevard right to the entrance.

Roseate Spoonbills *(opposite)*

Sometimes confused with that other pink bird, the flamingo, the magnificent Roseate Spoonbill is distinguished by its flat, spoon-shaped bill. Its long, fringed feathers once were prized for ladies hats. Roseates feed in the shallow muddy waters around Tampa Bay area mangroves at low tide. Their pink hues come from the crustaceans in their diet.

Sunshine Skyway Bridge *(above)*

Patterned after the Brotonne Bridge over the Seine River in France, The Bob Graham Sunshine Skyway is synonymous with St. Petersburg. The 15.5 mile-long bridge soars 190 feet over Tampa Bay. Its longest stay has 82 strands, weighs 37 tons, and is 1260 feet long.

Night Drama *(pages 110–111)*

Stunning cable-stay architecture, dramatic plays of light and shadow against blue sky, and dramatic nighttime up-lighting make driving across the Sunshine Skyway an exhilarating experience. Night or day, it is a favorite subject of artists and photographers.

Fish and Wildlife Research Institute *(top)*

Created in 2004, the Fish and Wildlife Research Institute is headquartered in St. Petersburg, with many field laboratories around the state. Under the auspices of the Florida Fish and Wildlife Conservation Commission, its mission is to study and help restore ecosystems, fisheries, wildlife and imperiled species, and to study red tides.

Museum of History *(bottom)*

St. Petersburg's Museum of History has 32,000 artifacts, 8,000-plus photos, and 5,000 documents preserving regional history. The museum is best known for its exhibit, *Flight One Gallery*, with its glass-enclosed First Airline Pavilion. The Flight One Gallery commemorates the world's first commercial flight between St. Petersburg and Tampa in 1914.

Salvador Dali Museum

With nearly 2,500 pieces, St. Petersburg's Salvador Dali Museum contains the world's most comprehensive collection of the famous surrealist's work, including his own museum in Figueres, Spain. The exciting family museum, which recently celebrated its first quarter-century, is growing rapidly; a new facility is planned for 2010.

St. Petersburg Yacht Club

Established in 1909, the St. Petersburg Yacht
Club in downtown St. Pete is known as the
"sailing capital of the south." SPYC has an
international reputation for its regattas and
youth sailing programs, which have pro-
duced collegiate All-American athletes.
Club members have included Olympic
and America's Cup champions.

Floating Chapel

St. Pete definitely is in the running as home of the world's most unique wedding chapel. The traditional church, with its tall stained glass windows and cathedral ceilings, floats on its own barge at The Pier and can set sail for the beach, the bay, or—if you live on the water—your own backyard.

The Coliseum

Some will recognize the historic, pink stuccoed, 1924 building in downtown St. Petersburg from scenes in the 1985 movie, Cocoon. The massive ballroom has one of the largest dance floors in America, with a capacity of 2000 people.

BayWalk

Trendy shops, martini and daiquiri bars, theme restaurants, and the 20-screen Muvico complex make up the $40 million BayWalk theme plaza in downtown St. Petersburg, part of the transformation of St. Pete from a sleepy retirement town to a vibrant, multi-generational city.

Muvico *(opposite)*

The mega-cool, mega-movie complex at BayWalk is one of 14 themed Muvico centers in Florida, with state-of-the-art digital technology, a new IMAX theater, childcare services, and full service restaurants. Its 20 stadium-seating auditoriums have an astounding 4,200-seat capacity.

Renaissance Vinoy *(above)*

A grande dame of the Gilded Age, the glamorous Renaissance Vinoy Resort is among Florida's finest examples of early 20th century Mediterranean Revival architecture. The St. Petersburg resort has its own private marina, an 18-hole golf course, tennis complex, and spa. Its restaurants and lounge are gathering spots for major league baseball superstars.

Don CeSar Hotel *(above and opposite)*

Rising like a pink-iced wedding cake on St. Pete Beach, "The Don" is the sweetest confection of the Gilded Age. With its palm-fringed entrance suitable for royalty, the Moorish-style flamingo-pink sand castle, trimmed with towers and spires, once hosted larger-than-life characters like F. Scott Fitzgerald and Al Capone.

Beach Elder

The ridges in the scallop shell at its base gives a perspective on the miniscule size of the beach elder blossom, which is nearly indiscernible to the casual observer. The beach elder bloom has a spike with dozens of tiny flower bracts.

Under the Boardwalks

Wooden boardwalks all along the coastline add a picturesque ambience while protecting the fragile dunes and beach vegetation from potential damage by foot traffic. The walkways also provide shelter and shade for small wildlife such as the threatened Florida Gopher Tortoise.

Rainbow Lorikeet *(opposite)*

Though it is native to Australia and Asia, the Rainbow Lorikeet thrives in its home at Tampa's Lowry Park Zoo. Visitors can buy a cup of nectar to feed the brilliant-hued parrots in the free-flight Lorikeet Landing aviary.

Sunken Gardens *(top and bottom)*

A century ago, a plumber named George Turner bought a Florida sinkhole, drained it and planted fruits, vegetables, and oak trees for shade. By 1920 he was giving nickel tours and selling his produce, which became so popular that by 1935 the price had elevated to 25 cents. In 1999 the mature four acres were acquired by the city of St. Pete.

Fort De Soto Park (above)

Dating back to the Spanish American War, the 1,136-acre Fort De Soto Park is comprised of five islands. The park's North Beach was awarded the coveted rating of the #1 Beach in America by "Dr. Beach," Dr. Stephen Leatherman. Park amenities and activities include guided nature walks, fishing piers, camping, picnicking, and war re-enactments.

Beaches of Tampa Bay (opposite)

Sugary white sands, aquamarine waters, and year-round blue skies make Tampa Bay one of the most desirable areas to live and vacation in America. Factor in colorful shore birds and profusions of tropical flowers, and Dr. Beach may just be compelled to retire the crown permanently to this slice of Paradise on the Gulf of Mexico.

Since 1989, Robert La Follette has been working as a graphic designer and photographer. His photographs have won numerous awards and have appeared in *Shutterbug Magazine, Informant Guest, and Creation Magazine*. La Follette is also a contributing writer and photographer for *Florida Wildlife Magazine*.

Robert was awarded Best of Show at the Boyd Hill Nature Photography Contest in St. Petersburg, Florida. He has been featured on "i On Tampa Bay" for PAX Television in Tampa. Robert's photography also appears around Tampa Bay, most notably with the Tampa Bay Convention and Visitors Bureau, where his images showcase the beauty and attractions that make Tampa Bay a world-renowned vacation destination. La Follette teaches creative photography online and in numerous photography workshops around the United States and Canada.

Robert lives in Tampa, Florida with his wife, Dawn, to whom he has been happily married for over 18 years. Wildlife enthusiasts, together they perform volunteer work with Tampa's Lowry Park Zoo and Clearwater Marine Aquarium. To view more of Robert's award- winning photography, please visit www.robertlafollette.com.

Karen T. Bartlett is an award-winning travel journalist whose work appears in books, magazines and newspapers throughout North America and the Caribbean. She made her home on the Gulf Coast of Florida two decades ago, and no matter how far she travels, she always looks forward to a joyful return.

www.karentbartlett.com